Ireland Travel Guide

Thomas Leon

Ireland Travel Guide

ISBN-13: 978-1974432707
ISBN-10: 197443270X

First Edition: August 2017
10 9 8 7 6 5 4 3 2 1

Thomas Leon

CONTENTS

Introduction

Booking a trip to Ireland is akin to experiencing a lifetime worth of adventures in one single trip. With ancient ruins, lively music, endless laughter and chatter, plus miles and miles of unspoiled beauty to explore, this Gaelic country is known as one of the most vibrant places in Europe, and for good reason. Boasting a medley of adventures, picturesque sights, lively music, excellent food and more importantly, some of the most glorious alcoholic beverages in the world, Ireland literally does offer something for just about everyone.

As an experienced traveler who has covered more countries than I care to count, I would never hesitate to recommend a trip to Ireland. The moment I set foot in this country and gazed in unabashed wonder at the vivid greenery around me, I knew I was in for a treat, but nothing could have prepared me for the delightful clash of colors, cultures and adventures that I was about to experience. A most pleasurable assault on the senses is how I would best describe a holiday in Ireland. From ringing silence to loud drunken chatter, to calm, crystalline waters clashing with the foamy waves and whipping against jagged rocks, Ireland is a contrast in itself.

In this book, I will provide you with up-to-date information about visiting this unique land. Join me in my quest to uncover hidden glacial fjords. Trek with me as I explore miles of greenery to see Game of Thrones® come to life in the original filming locations, or, better yet, come with me as I pub-crawl my way across Dublin, sampling some of the best lagers and whiskeys in the world. And don't forget to check out my list of practical information that will help make your stay in Ireland as comfortable as possible.

If you're worried that you can't afford accommodations in this remote European country, rest assured. As a veteran traveler, I've drawn up a list of different options that will fit just about any budget. From 5-star luxury resorts to comfortable hostels, or even glamping in the middle of nowhere, I can assure you that you'll find somewhere comfortable to lay your head at night. And, since no vacation is considered complete without a couple of shopping sprees, you may also want to check out my list of traditional Irish souvenirs that will remind you of your bygone adventures in Ireland.

Grab your hiking boots, your sense of adventure, your best camera and this book and I'll take you across one of the many hidden wonders of the world.

Chapter 1: Practical Information

Getting around

Depending on where you're staying, getting around Ireland can be quite easy. If you're staying in the larger cities and towns, you can easily travel by public buses which are cheap and reliable. Still, do bear in mind that the bus service in smaller towns and villages only operates a couple of times a week, so if you're staying in the countryside, I would certainly recommend that you rent your own car. You can always get around by taxi, but at the end of the day, renting your own vehicle can help you cut back on cost while giving you maximum flexibility.

Because Ireland is practically brimming with picturesque areas, it's also a good idea to rent a bike when you're exploring the countryside. This—at least according to me—is the best way to experience Irish villages and moors at their most natural advantage, complete with the balmy Irish breeze playing in your hair. A note of warning about rentals though—if you book from luxury resorts or hotels, you'll undoubtedly end up spending twice or even three times more than what you would pay to rent the same bike or car from an average guesthouse.

If time is of the essence to you, don't think twice about boarding an internal flight that will take you from one corner of Ireland to the other. While you'll undoubtedly miss out on some unique sights, this is the quickest way of ensuring that you reach your destination as quickly as possible. Alternatively, coaches and trains are other modes of transportation that I can certainly recommend if you're visiting Ireland, since you'll get to see plenty of green scenery as you whizz towards your destination. To cut back on costs, you can choose from different types of tickets, including: monthly, family day, monthly return, 5-day return, day return or single. If you're spending over a week in Ireland, you might consider getting a rail pass. The 8-day Irish Explorer pass, for example, costs about 160 euros, which is far cheaper than booking individual tickets.

Because Ireland is surrounded by small islets and islands that are well-worth a visit, ferries and boat shuttles are also quite popular as far as transportation is concerned.

Festivals and Events

It's no secret that the Irish love to party, so you can expect your fair share of festivals and events during your stay, regardless of how short it is.

If you're visiting Ireland in March for example, there's no escaping St Patrick's Day. This is when literally every village and town comes together in a raucous celebration filled with cheer, good humor, green ribbons, hats and clothes, without forgetting the booze of course. Think of it as the Irish version of America's 4th of July, but on a grander, noisier scale.

Other popular celebrations include the Irish Grand National, Wicklow Gardens Festival, Bloomsday, Irish Derby, Galway Film Fleadh, Oxegen Woxegen, Irish Open Golf Championship, Puck Fair, Kilkenny Arts Festival and the Wexford Opera Festival, among others.

Money saving tips

Of course, vacationing is all about indulgences and enjoying some added luxuries that you normally wouldn't allow yourself in your everyday life. Of course, you don't want to penny pinch during your vacation in Ireland. But take it from a recovering shopaholic—it's always a good idea to keep tabs on your spending, so you the rest of your holiday won't be less than it could be because you exhausted your savings too soon, leaving you grumpy and miserable.

Here are a few money-saving tips I found that helped me in Ireland:

Travel off season

Not only will your flight be less expensive, but you'll also benefit from interesting discounts in terms of car rentals and accommodations. In Ireland, the low season is mainly at the end of April, May and September. Don't forget that travelling off-season will also help you avoid the lines and crowds in the restaurants and tourist attractions.

Enjoy Early-Bird specials at dinner

One thing I noticed in Ireland was that most restaurants do have 'early-bird specials' that are not unlike 'happy hours.' Therefore, if you place your order before 7pm, you can be sure to enjoy a significant discount on your meal. Do remember that you will have fewer choices than if you order directly off the main menu after 7pm.

Choose your accommodation carefully

If you're a person who normally opts for a hotel, think again. One of the best things about Ireland is that it offers a whole plethora of alternative accommodation choices that can easily rival your hotel room rate. Airbnb's are excellent options, and you will certainly have your choice of rooms to choose from if you're staying in Galway, Kerry or Dublin. If you are staying in the countryside, do consider B&B's, inns or guesthouses. Not only are these establishments much cheaper, but you'll also be able to experience a more authentic unvarnished Irish culture thanks to your hosts.

Think about Heritage Cards

Okay, this is an absolute must if you want to curb your expenses while in Ireland. Issued by the OPW (Office of Public Works), Heritage Cards can be used for a period of 12 months and offer free entry to an incredible number of attractions, including 75 heritage sites.

Culture and Etiquette

To start off, let me assure you that the Irish do not stand on airs and graces. Quite on the contrary, this country often describes itself as the 'Land of Cead Míle Fáilte' which roughly translates as the land of a hundred thousand welcomes. In fact, this is a phrase that I saw inscribed behind the counter in several pubs and bars. And after going to Ireland on two separate occasions, I have to say that I quite agree.

As far as etiquette is concerned, most locals greet each other and tourists with a standard, 'How are you,' or 'How do you do?' To this you can reply, 'How do you do?' Since drinks are an integral part of Irish culture, you might find locals paying for your beer if you're visiting a pub, so the polite thing to do would be to pay for the next round.

Most, if not all of the locals that I've encountered were extremely friendly, so I was left with the impression that, unlike some of the other countries I've visited, tourists are extremely well-received in Ireland. Indeed, just share a lager or two with the locals and you're practically one of them!

Chapter 2: Top attractions in Ireland

Enjoy a pint (or two) in Dublin

If you want to immerse yourself in authentic Irish culture, there's no better way to do it than to spend a couple of days in Dublin, the country's capital. For me, visiting Dublin was like taking a huge breath of fresh air: there's something about this Viking city that beautifully blends the past with the present, providing you with a modern yet historic haven of tranquility. Not unlike New York- but without the hustle and bustle- Dublin is a multi-layered cosmopolitan city with an influx of kaleidoscopic hues and fresh flavors.

Here are my personal favorite things to do in Dublin:

Go Pub Crawling

You can't go to Dublin without indulging in some good old fashioned pub crawling. The good news is that you'll never run out of pubs to check out, and I do mean that literally. If you're a fan of beer, you might want to check out the Porterhouse, which is the oldest microbrewery pub in the capital. With reasonable prices, this particular pub specializes in lagers, ales and stouts, particularly the oyster stout which, believe it or not, is made from real oysters. To soak up all the booze, you can also check out their rustic pub food such as bangers and mash, or even a nice bowl of Irish stew.

It is no secret that Dublin pubs are notoriously noisy and animated, but if you'd like to enjoy a quieter atmosphere, head over to Grafton Street where you'll find Grogan—the establishment that has been hailed as 'Dublin's Drinking Institution.' With a shabby chic charm and a relaxed atmosphere, Grogan offers the ideal bolt-hole for visitors who want to enjoy a quiet, albeit beautifully boozed up dinner with friends and family.

Check out Old Jameson Distillery

So, in case you haven't figured it out yet, Dubliners love to drink. If you want to understand how the drinking culture started in this part of Ireland, head over to Bow Street for a tour of the Old Jameson Distillery, where you might even get to sample some of delectable homemade brews. According to our guide, whiskey literally translates to 'the water of life' in Irish, so you can be sure to enjoy quite a few free tastings during your tour! One of the most popular tourist landmarks in Dublin, Old Jameson Distillery is open every day. Tours cost around €15 per adult, and you should know that if you're planning on stocking up on beers and whiskeys to bring home, remember that the sale of alcohol is prohibited before 12.30pm on Sundays in accordance to Dublin licensing laws.

Party in the Temple (Bar, that is!)

Considered as the party corner of Dublin, rest assured that the Temple Bar is not an actual temple, or a bar for that matter, but more of a long avenue, not unlike Montmartre in Paris. A vibrant hub bursting with artistic vision, the Temple Bar is a personal favorite of mine. The atmosphere is eclectic, to say the least, with street art, independent galleries, and restaurants that stay open all night long. This is also where you'll be able to check out several cultural institutions, such as the Irish Film Archive, Ark Children's Cultural Centre and the National Photographic Archive, among others.

Some of the area's most sought-after pubs include Bad Bobs, Auld Dubliner, Foggy Dew, Quays Bar, and Czech Inn, as well as the Turk's Head. I can personally recommend the Auld Dubliner if you want to enjoy a lively and booze-filled Irish atmosphere complemented by traditional folkloric music.

Weave your way cross the Giant's Causeway

You might have seen it in magazines and books. You've definitely seen it in movies. But believe me when I say that nothing will prepare you for the awe-inspiring sight of seeing those mysteriously shaped basalt columns rise majestically up next to each other, somehow creating perfect interlocking pattern.

Located in Northern Ireland in County Antrim, the Giant's Causeway gathers around 40,000 basalt columns created by a volcanic eruption. Well, according to my guide, Cronan, the volcanic eruption story is a 'load of bollocks.' His words, not mine. In this region, locals believe that an ancient Gaelic giant by the name of Fionn Mac Cumhail was challenged to a fight and built the causeway so he could make his way across the Northern Channel to meet his adversary. Fact or Fiction? You decide.

Regardless of its origin, there's no denying that the Giant's Causeway is one of the most scenic places in Ireland and well worth a visit. While entry is entirely free, you can also enhance your experience by booking a tour or even a cruise that will let you admire this majestic place from afar.

Personally, I booked a 3-day adventure tour that took me across Ireland's Northern Coast, starting in Belfast where I got to explore the iconic Titanic attraction. Following that, we headed even further north and took the Causeway Coastal Route which, incidentally, is known as one of the most picturesque routes in the world. On our way to the Giant's Causeway, we got to explore the seaside village of Carrickfergus which houses a castle that is 12 centuries old, a sight that is well-worth a visit.

On the second day of our adventure towards the Giant's Causeway, we made a stop in the village of Antrim, where we enjoyed an invigorating walk in the walled gardens of Glenarm Castle. According to our guide, it the oldest garden in all of Ireland. Next stop for us was the Carrick-a-Rede rope bridge which, trust me, is not for the faint hearted! I am naturally adventurous, but even I felt nervous as took my first step on the wobbly, ancient-looking bridge that led us all the way across a gaping 24-m deep chasm and on towards a small islet. Believe me when I say you'll need your nerves for this particular adventure—but you won't regret it!

From the other end of the rope bridge, we only had to take a short drive before finally reaching the Giant's Causeway. If you want to take your Giant Causeway adventure still further, you can even book a boat trip that will take you far out into the sea so you can see the basalt columns from afar.

Enjoy the awe-inspiring beauty of the Cliffs of Moher

Another breathtaking landmark in Ireland, the Cliffs of Moher, is featured in its fair share of popular movies, including Harry Potter and the Princess Bride. I would absolutely recommend a visit to this iconic natural attraction. In my opinion, this place is best enjoyed off-season, otherwise you may have to fight your way through the crowds of tourists that flock to the Cliffs of Moher.

Personally, I visited the Cliffs of Moher as part of the 'Burren and Cliffs of Moher Geopark' tour that I booked. A world away from Dublin and its party-loving crowd, this tour will show you Ireland in all its glorious wilderness. This is Ireland at its most panoramic and natural, enabling you to experience the country's west coast in its rawest form. It's good to know that the Cliffs actually reach 702 feet high, treating you to an exceptional view of the foamy ocean. Like my guide said, this is the place to be if we want a generous slice of visual drama, Irish style!

You might want to bring some warm clothing if you're planning on visiting the cliffs though, even during summer. Because of the high altitude, it can get quite windy there. I wouldn't recommend the Burren and Cliffs of Moher Geopark tour for children or people with mobility issues, since there is plenty of walking involved. Of course, you can always rent a 4X4 to go there, but I personally wouldn't. If you ask me, the best way to completely submerge yourself into that truly majestic experience is to hike through the unblemished landscape.

With an altitude of 702 feet above sea level, the Cliffs of Moher loom high above Ireland's western moors and boast three main viewing points:

The South Platform: At the end of the South Platform,

you'll see the 'Hags Head,' a natural rock formation that bears an uncanny resemblance to a seated woman. This platform also offers the ideal viewpoint of the Cliff's puffin colony that lives on Goat Island—a stretch of grassy land that lies a short distance from the cliffs. Not far from the south platform you'll find the Cliffs View Café, where you can warm up with a nice mug of Irish coffee.

The North Platform: Located at the highest point on the Cliffs of Moher, the northern platform is also where you'll find the famous O'Brien's Tower. This viewpoint additionally offers perfect views of the Aran Islands, Galway Bay and the An Branan Mor Sea Stack, which houses razorbills and guillemots.

The Main Platform: Because it is more easily accessible, this is also the most crowded viewpoint and I wouldn't recommend it if you're visiting during peak seasons or hours. However, this platform does offer a view of the southern cliffs, so you might want to head there if you don't feel like hiking all the way towards the other end of the Cliffs of Moher. If it's not too crowded, you might even spot the Hag's Head from this viewpoint.

Places to eat around the Cliffs of Moher

If you're hiking to the cliffs, take it from me—you will be starving afterwards. I don't know if was because of the invigorating trekking session or that fresh mountain air, but we were exceptionally famished after our trip. And that's saying something considering I'd enjoyed a massive Irish fry-up just hours earlier.

Fortunately enough, several pubs, cafes and small restaurants have set up shop not far from the cliffs. Check out Danny Macs for barbecue, An Teach Bia for coffee and light fare, Vaughan's Anchor Inn for typical Irish pub food (I can recommend their fish and chips) or even the Tasty Station for traditional Italian dishes, right in the middle of Ireland!

See Game of Thrones® come to life in original filming locations

If you didn't know already, the Northern Coast of Ireland is among the most important filming locations for the iconic fantasy series, Game of Thrones.® Whether you want to check out the Dark Hedges that masquerade as 'The Kingsroad' in the series, or even the Larrybane Quarry that was featured as Renly's Camp, fans of GOT will certainly be able to watch their series come to life, right in front of their eyes.

Because of the overwhelming popularity of series, several agencies offer special Game of Thrones® tours across the northern coast of Ireland. Below are two of the most popular GOT-themed adventures in the country. And don't worry- they're entirely devoid of spoilers!

Castles of the Seven Kingdoms

Dating back to the medieval and Norman times, the castles featured as 'Castles of the Seven Kingdoms' in the series have rapidly turned into iconic landmarks in Ireland. I was fortunate enough to have been able to visit Shane's Castle, located In County Antrim and I have to say, as a dedicated GOT fan, seeing this castle up close did give me chills. Shane's Castle and its surroundings—including Lough Neagh—was actually used as backdrops in several scenes. Lough Neagh was even featured as the 'Summer Sea' in the series.

A bit further up north of Shane's Castle is found Carncastle, the building that was used to represent Moat Cailin. Unfortunately, we weren't allowed inside the castle but tourists are still allowed to visit the grounds and take pictures of the glorious scenery. If you'd like to check out the centuries-old ruin that was shown as Winterfell, head over to County Down where you'll also see Castle Ward, as well as Audley's Field that was depicted as Strangford Lough.

Games of Thrones Food Tour

If, like me, you happen to be both a GOT fan and a foodie, the Game of Thrones® ® Food Tour is definitely something that you'll want to do! I booked my tour with Glenara Elite and got to see most of the major filming locations, where we also got to sample the local cuisine, washed down by a triple. Or two.

We started the tour in Owens Bar, not far from Downhill Strand that was shown as Dragonstone Beach onscreen. This is where we got to sample some traditional Irish bread dipped in various infused oils before making our way to Fullerton Arms. This quaint pub serves typically local fares such as Seafood Chowder and Wheaten bread in true GOT fashion. Lastly, we made our way to Mry McBrides, which is located in Cushendun. There, we got to visit the area that masquerades as Braavos in the series, before capping off the evening with bottles of red Irish ale and an assortment of cheese.

Family Friendly Activities

A common and unfortunate misconception is that Ireland is full of wilderness, cliffs, stormy seas and other potentially hazardous areas that are unsuitable for kids. This couldn't be further from the truth. While there is no denying that Ireland boasts an almost majestic wilderness, the country offers plenty of activities and adventures for the whole family.

Explore faerie lands and Donkey Sanctuaries in Lough Gur

I have to admit, I was quite surprised to found Lough Gur much less crowded in comparison to other popular spots in Ireland. But if you ask me, Lough Gur is easily one of the most picturesque places in the country and well-worth a visit, especially if you're travelling with kids. You can start the day off the most famous stone circle in Ireland, which according to local myth, paves the way to a unique faerie land. In Lough Gur, you'll also get to explore archeological sites and castle ruins.

Not far from Lough Gur is found the only Donkey Sanctuary in Ireland. Not only is this place entirely free of charge but it will provide hours of entertainment for the kids while helping them understand the world of animal conservation. The sanctuary is always looking for volunteers to take the donkeys out for a walk or simply spend time with them, so there's no denying that your kids will have the time of their lives!

Butlers Chocolate Experience

Described as the ultimate chocolate discovery tour in the whole of Ireland, the Butlers Chocolate Experience will certainly evoke powerful chocolate cravings in both kids and adults alike. Luckily enough, you'll get to check out the gift shop at the end of the tour. Found in Dublin, the Butlers Chocolate Experience will take the entire family across a tour of the premises where you'll learn about the history of chocolate before visiting the actual factory where you'll see how the confectionaries are made. Best of all, you'll even get to try your hand at crafting your very own homemade chocolate to bring home as a personalized souvenir.

After your tour, you can conclude this memorable trip with one of Butlers Chocolate's signature hot chocolate drinks in the on-site café.

Discover the magical underwater wildlife at The National Sealife Centre

With over 24 incredible displays, there is no denying that The National Sealife Centre is one of the best family-friendly attractions in Ireland. Found in Wicklow, the Sealife Centre offers interactive exhibitions, most of which are especially designed for children. From seahorses to red-bellied piranhas or even cuckoo wrasses, the centre is especially renowned for its tropical shark lagoon where you will be able to view leopard and black tip reef sharks up-close.

Letterfrack Bay Water Tours

If you're visiting Galway with your family, you should definitely check out the Letterfrack Bay Water Tours. One of my personal favorite things to do in Ireland, this tour will take you across a marine trail in a glass-bottom boat, enabling you to embark upon a unique voyage of discovery. As we set sail across Ballinakill Harbour, we saw an amazing number of porpoises, dolphins, grey seals and even sea birds that weren't at all afraid to come close to us.

Thanks to the glass-bottom boats, this tour will also help you discover the type of underwater world that's normally only reserved for divers. I would strongly suggest that you book a tour when the tide is low, in fact, we were informed that lower tides provide the best underwater views. After that pleasurably lengthy sailing trip, you'll certainly feel a bit puckish, so you can head over to the Harbor Café which specializes in a variety of homemade Irish dishes, which you can enjoy as you admire wonderful views of Diamond and Twelve Bens mountain ranges.

Chapter 3: Ireland's Hidden Gems

If you'd like to get away from the touristy crowds and explore some of the most picturesque and remote places in the world, rest assured that Ireland has its fair share of hidden gems that you can uncover at your own pace. No rush. No bustle. And certainly no fighting your way through the crowds.

Discover incomparable beauty across the Wild Atlantic Way

Stretched across Ireland's southern coast are the five major peninsulas: Mizen, Sheep's Head, Beara, Iveragh and Dingle. Known as the Wild Atlantic Way, this area promises stupendous views that literally unfold at every turn of the road. The Southern peninsulas hold some of the best-kept secrets in Ireland—and some of the most striking places I've ever had the privilege of visiting. Whether you want to simply lie under the darkest skies in Europe and star gaze, take a cable car that will glide you over some of the most thunderous oceans in the world, or get up close with whales, you can be sure that the Southern Peninsulas will introduce you to the kind of scenery that you wouldn't even dare imagine:

Bray Head Tower: Where the world comes to a standstill

Located on Valentina Island, Bray Head Tower is found off the coast of southwestern Ireland in the middle of a deep blue, foamy ocean. Built in the middle of the Napoleonic War, this particular tower reflects the sense of desolation and emptiness that war brings. As you stand at the foot of the tower and gaze out into the vast ocean that seems to stretch on for miles, it is much too easy to feel disconnected from reality. If you're lucky enough, you might even spot a few whales gliding majestically amidst the waves.

The Force Awakens on Skelling Island

Another island located in the middle of Ireland's Wild Atlantic Way, Skelling Island is well-worth a visit if you want to feast your eyes upon primal Irish beauty. Indeed, this island is so exceptionally unblemished that it was even used as a prime filming location for Star Wars: The Force Awakens.

The first thought that came to me when our boat approached the island, was that this stretch of green and brown land seemed to pop out of nowhere, right in the midst of the ocean. Lashed by the ferocious elements of nature, Skelling Island is brimming with wildlife, and housed a colony of monks who sought refuge here during the war. If you'd like to learn more about the island's rich cultural past, do pay a visit to the Skelling Heritage Center. Yes, I know a history lesson isn't exactly what you might have planned for your vacation, but trust me when I say it's worth it. For a more challenging experience, you can even try to climb up the 600 stone steps that lead to the monastic village, where you will be treated to a sweeping view of the mainland.

Driving the Wild Atlantic Way

If you've got time to spare, you can explore all of the 2,500km of the Wild Atlantic Way by car. Boasting an enigmatic, almost eclectic character, this region is brimming with coastal roads that were described by Chris Evans as the best roads he'd ever driven upon. And after experiencing this unique road trip for myself, I have to agree.

While you can of course trace your own Wild Atlantic

Way road trip, you can go on the most common routes if you'd like to save time. These include: Slea Head Drive, Kinsale to Clonakilty, Burren Beauty Drive, Ennis to Doonbeg, and Galway to Westport, as well as Glengesh Pass.

Secret Wonders in the Colclough Walled Garden

This place is such a well-kept secret in Ireland that I probably wouldn't have found it, had it not been for the group of locals that joined us for a pint in a small countryside pub in Wexford. This historic Georgian garden was originally created at the very beginning of the 19th century, and underwent intensive restoration back in 2010. From what we were told, all the restorative work was done in such a way so as to preserve the original structure and layout. I can assure you that you can certainly feel the rich history this place holds.

The Colclough Walled Garden is just a short walk away from Tintern Abbey, another historic building quite popular in the region. You can follow the same narrow woodland path that the Abbey's original inhabitants used to take when heading down to the garden. My first impression of the place was that time stood still—including the ruins of the old groundkeeper's cottage. An artfully built wall separates the grounds into two sides—the West, which is basically a kitchen garden; and the right, which bears ornamental plants. You'll also find five bridges in this garden, under which a small, softly-gurgling stream passes by.

Out of the two sections, I quite preferred the kitchen garden which did bring to mind the old 'garden to table' tradition that once existed in Tintern Abbey. The ornamental side was brimming with trees and herbaceous borders, as well as endless stretches of both perennial and annual flowers. Do try to visit in the summer when the flowers burst into life in a dizzying array of hues.

Admission is incredibly cheap at 3 euros (around $3.50), and the garden is open from 10am to 4pm from October-April, and 10am to 6pm from May to September. The Colclough Walled Garden is maintained by local volunteers who are extremely chatty and always eager to answer any question you might have, so don't hesitate to visit with them!

After touring the garden, you can check out the Abbey ruins, as well as the perfectly preserved antique buildings around it. From the carved stones to the heads that have been sculpted directly into the walls, there's plenty to do and see at the Abbey. Admission is around 4 euros per adult, but if you have a Heritage Card, you can go in for free. Parking and restrooms are available on site.

Explore different adventures at the Delphi Adventure Resort

Described by the locals as an Irish treasure, Delphi Adventure Resort in Galway is the ideal place to head if you're travelling with friends or family. With an extensive number of activities, this place embodies everything that Ireland stands for—fun, wonderful scenery, and even more fun. Indeed, from mountain-related activities to cycling, as well as several land and water activities, we honestly didn't have enough hours in the day to do everything. If you want to extend your adventure, rest assured that the Delphi resort offers a variety of accommodation types with something for every budget.

If you ask me, the Delphi Adventure Resort is one of the best ways to explore remote Irish areas and experience the very best of what the country has to offer, especially if you're short on time since you get to do so many things in just one place. For example, this establishment is known for its water activities that will take you out on those foamy seas as you enjoy a unique view of Galway from afar. I quite enjoyed the Sea Kayaking Tour, where we not only got to explore the shores of Connemara, but also Killary Harbour, which is one of the three glacial fjords in the country. This is definitely the adventure to book if you want to enjoy a thrilling new perspective on Ireland as you feast your eyes over dramatic mountain peaks, coastal birds and local mussel farms from your own private perch in the middle of the ocean.

If you're a bit of an adrenaline junkie, you might want to book the resort's mountain bike adventure. Ideal for anyone who wants a quick getaway from the hustle and bustle of the city, this adventure takes you across the untainted landscape around the resort as you ride alongside experienced instructors. Bikes and safety equipment are provided.

And to cool off after this thrilling adventure, you can book a traditional Irish body massage at the Delphi Spa, where the Thermal Suite only uses mountain water from the nearby ranges.

Glacial Fjords and more

This may be one of the best-kept secrets in Ireland. While glacial fjords are normally associated with places such as Norway and Iceland, Iceland does have three different fjords, one of which acts as a border between County Galway and County Mayo. Offering sublime photo opportunities, the fjords of Ireland can offer quite a striking sight, especially when flanked by imposing mountain ranges that are partially clouded by fog.

Cruise across the Killary Fjord

Get up close and personal with the most striking of all three fjords as you take a leisurely cruise across the crystalline waters of Killary. While we opted for a regular speedboat in order to cut back on costs, you can also book a catamaran cruise, where you will enjoy a hot lunch with Irish coffee and live music. If luck is on your side, you might even spot a couple of dolphins jumping out of the water. In less windy weather conditions, the water is actually so clear that you might even see a perfect reflection of the mountain ranges stretching cross the fjord.

Explore the rugged coastline

Killary Fjord is surrounded by a vast history—in the literal sense of the word. After our cruise, we took a long hike across the rugged coastline and made it into the small village of Leenane, which was actually featured in the movie, 'The Field.' In this village, you will find the Sheep and Wool Centre as well as a small museum where you'll be able to learn all about the wool commerce in Connemara. It even comes with a café and a gift shop if you'd like some handmade woolen artifacts to bring back home.

If you're up for a long nature walk, follow the grass-covered road (known to locals as the Green Road) that borders the fjord. This road was built back in the 19th century as part of a Famine Relief project and it now serves as a memorial to this devastating part of Irish history. At the end of the road you'll find the ruins of a small community where philosopher Ludwig Wittgenstein came to live after World War II. The cottage and field ruins along with the poignant stillness that lies in this region stands as testimony of all the hardships that this region once had to endure.

Fjord Farming

Head over to Killary Harbour where you'll be able to see mussels being farmed right in the pure fjord waters. Indeed, the harbor is one of the most important aquaculture centers in Ireland and if you visit this place in the morning, you might even see fishermen unloading fresh salmon and mussels on the dock. I was also pleasantly surprised to see a flock of different bird species both above and in the water, such as ringed plovers, grey herons, barnacle geese, and whopper swans, as well as tufted and mallard ducks.

Chapter 4: Accommodation in Ireland

Live in the lap of luxury

Yes, Ireland might be full of striking wilderness, but that doesn't necessarily mean you have to rough it up. Quite on the contrary, if you can afford it, it is well worth checking into one of the many accommodation choices you'll find in Ireland.

Currarevagh Country House

If you're a fan of Victorian décor, you'll undoubtedly be just as enthralled by Currarevagh Country House as I was when I first stepped into the gloriously elegant hall.

Bordering Lough Corrib, with plenty of woodland around, this establishment towers beautifully over a pristine environment, ideal for those seeking some peace and quiet in the midst of opuleint luxury. There's something about the atmosphere that echoes the bygone days that once formed part of Ireland's Victorian past.

I have to admit, I quite enjoyed the generous pampering from the meticulous staff who would go the extra mile—quite literally—to accommodate just about any request. The Currarevagh Country House only features 12 bedrooms, guaranteeing privacy and intimacy. Most of these rooms overlook the Northern mountain ranges or Lough Corrib. In this luxury guest house, you will also find several sitting rooms with open-turn fireplaces where you will be able to seek solace from the cold as you sip on a mug of cocoa. We were greeted each morning with a lavish Edwardian-style breakfast that was artfully laid out on the sideboard.

More importantly, Currarevagh Country House offers a wide variety of activities—some of which are quintessentially Irish, such as croquet. Because of its proximity to the Aran Islands, the front desk can also arrange for day trips, complete with picnic lunch. Or, why not hire a horse and a guide from the nearby equestrian center and feel the sea breeze in your hair as you gallop down the beach in Connemara?

Other nearby activities include Galway's numerous festivals such as the Oyster Festival (early September), Arts Festival (July), and the Galway Race Week (early August). Additionally, I quite enjoyed our day trip to The Burren, a unique attraction which is around an hour away from Currarevagh Guesthouse. The Burren has over 300 square kilometers of exposed limestone, bringing a rather mystical, and somewhat eerie, feel to the place. This area is also known for its rich botanical garden that houses over 700 different species of plants. If you're feeling particularly adventurous, you can also book an underground hike in the nearby Ailwee Caves.

The Fitzwilliam Hotel Dublin

Nestled in the very heart of Dublin is the Fitzwilliam Hotel which—to my great delight—is right next door to the Opera House. If you ask me, grand is the term that can best be used to describe this establishment. We couldn't really spend more than two days there—it does come at a price after all—but if you really want to take a break from reality for a while and just let yourself be enveloped by luxury, this is the place to be.

While countryside hotels tend to have a more refined and Victorian style, the Fitzwilliam Hotel Dublin has been entirely conceived to reflect the city's playful and contemporary ambiance. Because it is aptly located near some of the major establishments in Dublin, you can certainly grab a quick dinner in one of the many pubs. However, if you can afford to splurge, I would absolutely recommend at least one three-course dinner in the hotel's gastronomic restaurant. Or you can also enjoy a spot of high tea which includes both savory and sweet treats alike. To jazz things up a little, you can even ditch the tea altogether and get mimosas or champagne instead! (And yes, that is precisely what we did!)

Rooms are airy and spacious, most of them overlooking the city. Our room had a private balcony which we quickly turned into our own private perch for people-watching. Conveniently, WiFi was entirely free! Nearby attractions, or at least those that are within walking distance, include: Wild Wicklow Tour, Temple Bar, Guiness Storehouse, Dublin Castle and Trinity College.

Vacation like the royals in Ashford Castle

This historic Irish castle lies on a massive estate that measures 350 acres, providing the perfect holiday retreat as you indulge in the high life. Set on the calm shores of Lough Corrib, this castle has an impressive history that stretches over several centuries. This castle offers over 83 wonderfully decorated rooms that combine typical antique architecture with contemporary amenities. Dinner, for example, is served in an opulent George V dining room, while High Tea can be enjoyed in the Park Lounge that overlooks the countryside.

As far as activities are concerned, guests can enjoy the 9-hole golf course, falconry school, equestrian center and fishing.

Mid-Range options for families

If you're travelling with the whole family, chances are you'll want to stay in a kid-friendly establishment that will accommodate both your needs as well as those of the kids. Luckily enough, there are plenty of mid-range hotel options for families—with or without children!

Bunratty Castle Hotel

Okay, tell me what kid doesn't want to wake up in a legit Irish castle every day? Luckily enough, this is made possible through the Bunratty Castle Hotel. Located in the striking countryside of Bunratty, this hotel is ideal for those who want to explore the Western Irish countryside; indeed, the hotel is a short distance from the Burren, Cliffs of Moher as well as the 15th century old Burratty Castle and Folk Park.

As a guest of the hotel, you can choose between various types of accommodation, including a whole array of suites as well as deluxe or executive rooms. More importantly, it offers plenty of activities for the entire family, such as long walks in the countryside as you inhale the kind of pure air that can only be experienced away from the bustle of the city. Parents can enjoy a moment of bliss in the castle's Angsana Spa that offers several types of packages, including an overnight stay with a typical Irish breakfast the following morning. Some of the more popular treatments—and my personal favorites—include, the Angsana Indulgence which is comprised of body polish, massage, facial, lunch, hands and foot treatments; as well as the Ayu-Reverie, which blends an Indian head massage with an hour-long Ayurvedic massage.

In terms of food, the castle has three restaurants for you to choose from. I can personally recommend that you check out 'The Library' which is an actual old-fashioned library where breakfast is served every morning. And if you've got fussy kids, fret not. The castle does offer children's menus, and meals can be customized according to personal preferences, for adults and children alike.

Ferndale Luxury Bed and Breakfast

If you want to get away from it all, there's no better place to do it than Ferndale Luxury Bed and Breakfast. What sets this mid-range establishment apart is that it's set on Achill Island which is off the west coast of Ireland. Accessible by boat shuttle or ferry, this B&B felt more like some kind of ultra-comfortable guesthouse to me, so warm and welcoming were our hosts. Surrounded by a vivid green landscape that clashes beautifully with the bright blue sky, it's hard not to feel disconnected from the hustle and bustle of your everyday life as you enjoy your stay on this charming island.

What I loved the most about this B&B was how each room comes with a theme. You can choose between the Roman Palaestra (Royal Suite), Arabian Nights (Luxury Double Room), Ancient China (Deluxe Double Room), Gothic Courtyard (Standard Double Room), and Mayan Treasure Bay (Mini Suite), as well as the Laguna Veneta (Junior Suite). Breakfast is served in a spacious dining room that provides the perfect setting for everyone to mingle and socialize with both local guests and tourists. Along with a traditional Irish breakfast, you can also choose from fresh fruit platters, porridges, Greek-style yogurt or even a cheeseboard platter with varying selections.

Ballyvolane House

Brimming with typical Irish warmth and hospitality, Ballyvolane House is ideal for anyone who wants to enjoy a relaxing retreat in the North Cork countryside. The best thing about this particular accommodation is that it offers a variety of options in terms of sleeping arrangements. For example, if you're visiting the region during summer, you can also opt for glamping in their garden, which offers a comfortable twist on traditional camping.

These 4-metre bell tents can easily accommodate 2 people, but if you're travelling with kids, you can also opt for the 5-metre tents that can sleep up to 2 adults and 2 children. All meals are provided in the main house. And don't worry, you won't be roughing it up on the ground either—the tents have been fitted with timber beds and comfortable mattresses that are covered with soft cotton sheets, blankets and duvets. More surprisingly, you'll even find an antique-style chandelier that hangs from the 'ceiling' to provide both warmth and light. Rest assured that the tents are properly furnished with chairs, carpets and even bedside tables. A traditional Irish wash house is found a very short distance from the glamping area, where you'll find showers, toilets, clothes-hooks, hair-dryers and mirrors.

Budget friendly accommodation for solo travelers and couples

The good thing about Ireland is that there's always an option for everyone, regardless of budget. Therefore, if you don't want to spend a lot, rest assured that there are still plenty of options of you in terms of accommodation. Backpackers might want to stay in hostels, where they can choose between shared dormitories or individual rooms. Alternatively, you'll find a whole range of glamping sites, B&B's or even budget hotels that will suit couples, small families and solo travelers alike.

Isaacs Hostel

Located in Dublin, Isaacs Hostel has been described as one of the friendliest establishments in Ireland—and I can totally vouch for that. Because it is found at the very heart of Dublin, you'll find that most of the major attractions as well as pubs and restaurants are found within walking distance to the hostel. In spite of its affordable rates, Isaacs Hostel offers free WiFi, free breakfast, free sauna facilities and even a variety of free events and festivals that will immediately put you in the mood to party.

With prices as low as $16 per person, this hostel offers single, double/twin, triple or even four-bed rooms for families. Facilities include central heating, bed linens, shared bathrooms, key-card access and towels. If you'd like to save up even more, you can always opt for the shared dormitories that start at around $10 per person. Dormitories have between 4, 6, 8, 10, 14 or 16 beds and you can choose between male, female or mixed rooms. My friends and I did opt for the 14 room mixed dormitory just for the experience, and believe me when I say that this was an experience like none other. Strangers from all over the world mingled easily as we swapped stories, traded travel tips and sipped from our bottles of chilled Irish lager.

Lough Owel Lodge

If you're travelling with children, I would certainly recommend a stay at the Lough Owel Lodge. Located in Westmeath County, this quintessentially Irish farm offers various types of activities in spite of its budget-friendly rates. Bird watching, for instance, is quite a popular hobby in the region, given the sheer number of trees and bushes that dot the emerald green countryside. In fact, not far from the farmhouse is a small lake where tourists often gather with binoculars to try and spot some of the rare bird species that are unique to the country. Additionally, the lodge can also arrange for other types of activities such as the popular 'Ireland East,' 'Great Escapers,' as well as the 'Old Rail Trail' tours.

Each room at the Lough Owel Lodge is named after one of the lakes in the region. Guests can choose between Lough Sheelin (twin room), Lough Lene (double room), Lough Ennell (double room), Lough Owel (double room) or the Family Room, Lough Derravaragh.

The House Hotel

Located in the liveliest part of Galway, the House Hotel boasts retro-style fixtures and bold shades. Best of all, the rooms are entirely sound-proof which might provide some solace from the all-night parties that often happen in the neighborhood. With a surprisingly affordable price tag in spite of its comfort and amenities, the House Hotel is set in a century-old stone building that also houses a bistro where you can enjoy contemporary twists on traditional Irish fares.

Guests can choose between various types of rooms. While the suite is undoubtedly more expensive, the standard room is quite affordable and consists of two full beds or a king bed, WiFi, hair dryer and security deposit box.

Chapter 5: Eat (and drink) like the Irish!

We all know that good food starts with good ingredients. And if you've been to Ireland, you would have seen for yourself that produce couldn't get any fresher—especially in the countryside.

A word of advice—do bring some spare jeans with elastic waistbands on your trip to Ireland. You're gonna need them.

Enjoy over 50 types of Irish cheeses

Yes, I know. Ireland doesn't really evoke the same cheese fantasies as France does. Which is exactly why I was stunned to discover that Ireland actually produces some of the best types of cheese that I've ever tasted anywhere in the world—including France and Italy. According to our guide, cheese-making in Ireland actually dates back to monastic times but only soared in popularity in the 70's.

If you ask me, the best places to sample Irish cheeses are Kells, Galway and Dublin, where you can find over 50 different varieties. Both Galway and Dublin often host wine and cheese evenings where you can learn about the best types of pairings. I was actually able to attend one such evening in Dublin, at the Fallon & Bryne pub. We were served a variety of charcuterie and cheese, both of which were accompanied by several glasses of local and imported wine. If you're not on a restricted budget, do consider spending the night back in Dromoland Castle, where breakfast consists of a full Irish cheeseboard which you can sample on an optional piece of freshly baked, crusty baguette.

A Culinary Journey across Ireland's Ancient East

What better way to seamlessly blend your Irish vacation into a culinary discovery than to explore the magnificent wonders of Ireland's Ancient East? Trace a route from County Cork to County Meath as you head off to uncover some of the most delectable dishes in Ireland, sprinkled with a hefty dose of history. Along this route, you'll also find a wealth of farmer's markets that are practically bursting with fresh produce, lush green counties, succulent slabs of meats and the type of ripe fruits that practically gush with juice upon the first bite.

In fact, if you're an avid foodie, why not book the famous two-nights Food and Heritage Trail? This adventure charts a route across Ireland's Ancient East and takes you all the way from Waterfort into Kilkenny as you indulge in some of the most gourmet dining experiences in the country. Enjoy a personal tasting tour of local distilleries, and enjoy samples of Irish gin and cider as you kick off the adventure in Waterford, where you will also get to sample the world-renowned traditional bread known as Waterford Blaa. After dinner, you will have the chance to enjoy some Granville Whiskey Wall as a delectable nightcap.

The following day sees you in Walsh's Bakehouse for some local pastries and coffee, before moving on to a gourmet dinner in Bodega restaurant. And as you reach your destination on the third and last day, you will be able to sample a traditional Irish breakfast which includes Bubble and Squeak, grilled tomatoes, eggs, mushrooms, baked beans, sausages, bacon, tea, toast and marmalade. And if you're brave enough to try it—a side of black pudding.

Drink like the Irish!

There's no doubt that Irish whiskey is actually among the most popular spirits in the world—and for good reason. While notoriously expensive around the world, the good news is that, in Ireland, you will be able to sample over 200 different brands of local whiskey at a highly affordable price. If you simply want a taste of each brand, I can suggest tasting tours at the Teeling Whiskey Distillery (Dublin) and Dingle Distillery (County Kerry).

I personally wanted to stock up on a few bottles to bring back home, so our guide in Dublin took us to the Celtic Whiskey Shop, which stocks some of the rarest types of whiskey in the world. Best of all? They actually let you sample the drink before buying it, so you can be sure there won't be any nasty surprises when you get it home. If you're a serious whiskey enthusiast, you can also check out the 2-day whiskey school at the Dingle Distillery.

Must-try Irish Dishes

Below are just a few of the traditional Irish dishes that I wouldn't hesitate to recommend:

Sticky Toffee Pudding

I'll be the first to admit that I don't have much of a sweet tooth. With a penchant for savory food, I was quite hesitant to try what initially sounded like an overly-sweet treat to me. After some persuading, however, I grabbed my spoon and dove right in. I was a convert at first bite. This typically Irish dessert basically consists of an exceptionally moist slice of sponge cake, slathered with toffee sauce and served with a scoop of vanilla ice cream. One of the most decadent desserts I've ever tasted, this is definitely not a diet-friendly treat!

Irish Lobster

This was another pleasant surprise to me since lobster didn't exactly jump to mind when I thought of Ireland. In Dublin, however, we went into this pub that served up exquisitely fresh, soft and buttery lobster that was delicately placed back into the shell after cooking and served alongside several thick slices of buttered Irish soda bread.

Irish fry-up

The local cure for hangovers, these fry-ups are often served for breakfast or brunch. A heaping plate consists of generous servings of buttered toast, beans, grilled tomatoes, rashers, Irish sausage and an egg, sunny-side up! Accompanying that is a slice of black pudding, also known as blood pudding. If, like me, you don't have the guts to try this typically Irish delicacy, rest assured that its blood-free counterpart (white pudding) is also available in most places.

Soda bread

This is so popular in Ireland that various families have added their own twists to the original recipe. While the basic ingredients are baking soda, buttermilk, and flour, some establishments choose to enhance the classic recipes by adding oats, bran, seeds, sugar, dried fruits or even honey to the dough before baking it. It is often enjoyed warm, with liberal slathering's of butter.

Chapter 6: Indulge in some shopping, Irish-style

I have to say, shopping in Ireland is quite an experience.

While the country derives a solid portion of its income from the tourism industry, you won't find a lot of the typical souvenirs that you might find in other countries—at least not in the rural regions that we've explored. On the contrary, the Irish believe that the best way to embody their country's spirit and culture is through its food, drink and music—three of the main things you will undoubtedly encounter when shopping for souvenirs.

Here are some typical souvenirs you can expect to bring back from Ireland:

Chocolate

Fret not, these are not your usual duty-free chocolates that one normally grabs in a hurry to distribute as souvenirs. Irish chocolate—or at least the ones filled with delicious Irish liqueur—is an art in itself. I can personally recommend local chocolatiers such as The Chocolate Garden which is found in Wicklow. If you're visiting the Ring of Kerry, do give the Skelligs Chocolate Factory a try.

Mead

Okay, I'll admit. Irish mead is an acquired taste, but once you get past the unexpected sweetness of it all, it does make for an excellent nightcap, especially on those glacial winter nights. This honey wine is traditionally served to the newly married couple at weddings, because it was once thought to enhance the powers of fertility and virility. According to local legends, the term 'honeymoon' actually originated from an old Irish tradition where guests used to gift the couple enough of the honey-based beverage to last for an entire moon cycle.

Irish Moonshine

Yes, it was once pronounced illegal in Ireland. But rest assured that this beverage—locally known as Potcheen—is now legal in various part of the country and can be bought in small pot stills in most pubs. Quick warning though—it does contain 40%-50% alcohol by volume, so you do want to exert caution.

Ketty Glass

County Kerry is especially known for its hand-blown glass factories where various types of sculptures are swirled with vivid blue and green hues.

Bodhrán

A nod to the rich musical culture of Ireland, Bodhrán refers to an Irish drum which is made from goat skin and wood, and is normally decorated with traditional Celtic symbols.

Whiskey and Lager

Well, that's a given. You can't exactly leave Ireland without bringing home some locally-brewed lager and whiskey now, can you?

Irish Crystals

Few people know that Ireland makes some of the most

exquisite crystal sculptures in the world. If you would like to bring some Irish crystal home, you can check out the Waterford Crystal Factory, which is known for its wonderful collection of crystal homewares. From Dungarvan bows to Crosslake Wine sets, or even carafes, vases, pitchers, and more, this is the place where you can be sure to find just about anything made from Irish crystal. Just be sure to ask for a crash-proof packaging. For expensive crystal items, it's also a good idea to enquire about warranties or insurance.

Conclusion

Ireland is such a vast land, and filled with so many natural attractions that it can be hard to arrange your schedule in such a way as to drink everything in. This is why I would absolutely recommend a lengthy vacation in this country where the striking greenery clashes so masterfully with the vast blue that surrounds it.

Even if you're not trying to curb your expenses, I would also suggest that you spend at least a couple of nights in a family-owned inn or B&B in order to experience the unique Irish warmth and hospitality for yourself. Devoid of stuffy formality, the Irish have a way of making you feel like you're one of theirs, and most of the locals that I've encountered went above and beyond in making our stay as enjoyable as possible.

Ireland is the kind of country where you can sit in a crowded pub and partake in playful banter with the locals as you enjoy pint after pint of local lager; or, enjoy the striking sense of isolation that comes as you stand alone at the edge of the Cliffs of Moher. This is the moment where all of your senses are invigorated as striking scenery stretches out for miles at your feet, and the warm Irish sun plays in your hair. Later, you can head into a family-owned restaurant for dinner, where you will be serenaded by local bands playing traditional Celtic music as you tuck into juicy slabs of meat and large slices of soda bread.

Indeed, if you want a holiday rich in culture, contrast and color, don't think twice about making Ireland your next holiday destination. I can promise it will be well worth it.

Thank you so much for reading this book. I hope it's useful for you.

If you like the book, would you please do me a huge favor and write me a review on Amazon? I would really appreciate it and look forward to reading your review.

Best

Thomas

Check out my travel books...

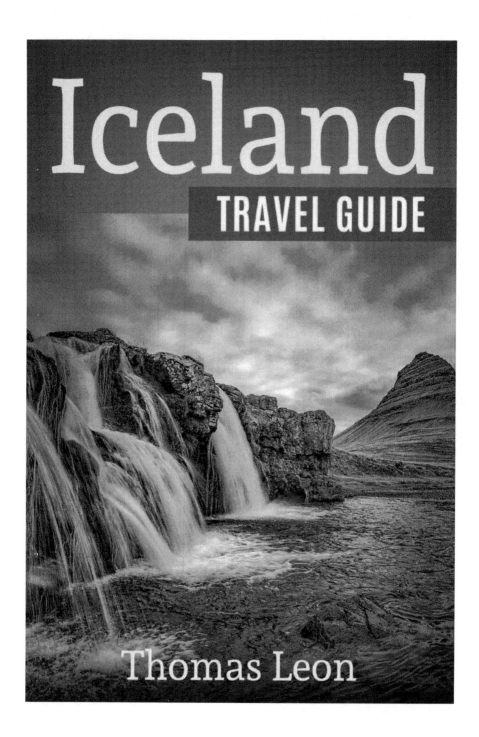

Iceland

TRAVEL GUIDE

Thomas Leon

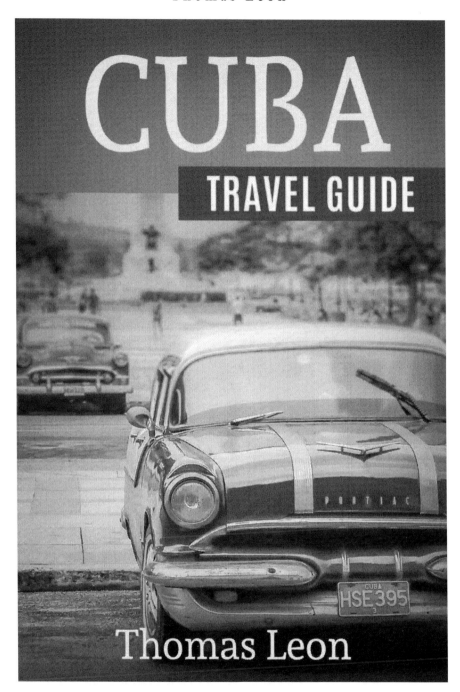

Hawaii

TRAVEL GUIDE

Thomas Leon

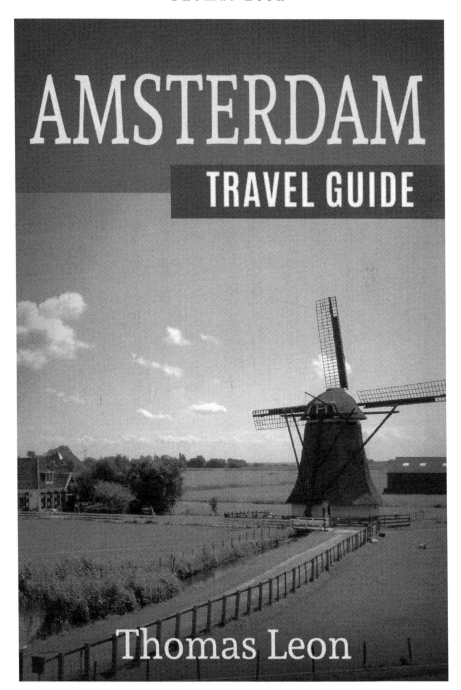

AMSTERDAM

TRAVEL GUIDE

Thomas Leon

Made in the USA
Middletown, DE
10 January 2018